Come See and Wonder

Come See and Wonder

by

Wyneth Nobbs

Come, See and Wonder

by Wyneth Nobbs

Text - copyright © Wyneth Nobbs 2024

Photos - copyright © Wyneth Nobbs 2024, except

Dapper Little Gent (p 8) - copyright © Jennifer Scott 2022

Eastern Water Dragon (p.10) - copyright © Kat McKinnon 2024

Hungry 'Juvenile' Eastern Koel and Little Wattlebird (p.25) - copyright © Julie Pallant 2024

Cover design by Don Emms.

All rights reserved

This book or parts thereof may not be reproduced in any form, stored in a retrieval system, or transmitted in any form by any means - electronic, mechanical, photocopy, recording or otherwise - without prior written permission of the publisher and copyright holder.

No AI Training: Without in any way limiting the author's exclusive rights under copyright, any use of this publication to "train" generative artificial intelligence (AI) technologies to generate text is expressly prohibited. The author reserves all rights to license uses of this work for generative AI training and development of machine learning language models.

Scripture quotations marked (NIV) are taken from the Holy Bible, New International Version®, NIV®. Copyright © 1973, 1978, 1984, 2011 by Biblica, Inc.™ Used by permission of Zondervan. All rights reserved worldwide. www.zondervan.com The "NIV" and "New International Version" are trademarks registered in the United States Patent and Trademark Office by Biblica, Inc.™

Scripture quotations marked (ERV) are taken from the Holy Bible: Easy-to-Read Version (ERV), International Edition © 2013, 2016 by Bible League International and used by permission.

Published by Nenge Books, Australia, September 2024

Desktop and design by Nenge Books, ABN 26809396184

www.nengebooks.com

email: nengebooks1@gmail.com

Nenge Books is a publishing service provider assisting independent authors to publish using cost effective print-on-demand technology. Enquiries from authors are welcomed.

ISBN 978-0-6459597-5-8

Contents

List of Photos	vii
Acknowledgements	ix
Introduction	xiii
Prologue	xvi
The Circus in the Tree	1
The Dapper Little Gent	5
Face to Face	9
'Wattle' They Do Next?	14
Juvenile's Story	19
The Rescue Mission	26
A Simple Delight	31
Interesting Web Sites	42
Endnotes	43

Orchard Swallowtail Butterfly

Blue-tongue Lizard

List of Photos

My front garden	Cover
Orchard Swallowtail Butterfly	vi
Blue-tongue Lizard	vi
Two King Parrots	viii
Juvenile Blue-faced Honeyeater	xi
Eastern Rosella	xiv
Black-faced Cuckoo-shrike	xviii
Rainbow Lorikeet in flight	1
Hungry Rainbow Lorikeet	2
Upside down Rainbow Lorikeet	4
Red-backed Fairy-wren[1]	8
A Juvenile Eastern Water Dragon[2]	10
Adult Little Wattlebird	15
Obedient Juvenile Little Wattlebirds	18
Feeding time	20
Hungry 'Juvenile' Eastern Koel and Little Wattlebird[3]	25
The Snake Whisperer in action	27
The Diamond Python	28
Pair of doves choosing their nest site	32
Patient parent on nest duty	33
Dove feeding chicks	34
Who is going first?	35
Spotted Dove on windowsill	36
Peaceful Spotted Dove nesting	39

Two King Parrots

Acknowledgements

I am delighted to acknowledge the efforts of the people who played an integral part in making this book possible.

I have been astounded by the gracious and encouraging feedback from the readers of my first book, *A Garden of Simple Delights & Profound Truths*. My first thanks go to you. Your comments cheered me on when writing this book became tedious, as the words failed to come and the sentences just wouldn't fall into place.

Many thanks go to my precious and trusted friends who were willing to help in the repetitive and exacting process of proof-reading numerous drafts of this book. Each proof-reader has brought to the task their own gifts such as patience, honesty, and love, as well as their individual styles, skills, and background expertise. They have also sacrificed large chunks of their time to read the drafts, make corrections and pray. Grant and Kath, Terry and Ros, and Jennifer live locally. They plied me with cups of coffee and sometimes a meal as we thrashed out grammar, punctuation, word meanings, paragraph relocation, deletions and additions.

Geoff and Judy, who live in another locality, gave their feedback and corrections over the phone. Don and Diane also live in a different locality. Returning home after a weekend away, they called by my place to give their proofreading feedback. They willingly gave their time, knowing full well that the last few hours of their homeward journey would be in the dark. I thank God for each of them.

Some very special individual acknowledgments are due to Judy, Jennifer and Don. Judy willingly tackled the first very rough draft, yet still managed to come up with an insightful critique that only a dear friend of many years could do. Jennifer very graciously got out her paints and painted a charming picture of the 'Dapper Little Gent' when there was no photo to be found amongst our photo collections. Don used his skills as a graphic artist to design the colourful and inviting front cover. Thank you all for your special help.

I had recorded the majority of non-human visitors to my garden through the lenses of my very ordinary cameras. Most photos were taken years before this book was a vague idea in my mind. They were taken on impulse rather than planned compositions. When viewed on the computer, these photos show up well but unfortunately, when in print, the quality of some photos is not as good. Once again Jennifer very generously combed through her photos to fill in the gaps in my photo collection. She also commandeered the help of her niece, Kat, to photograph some eastern water dragons. Jennifer also contacted Julie from a Facebook Group, North Coast Birds and Wildlife, to acquire copyright permission to use her amazing photo of a young eastern koel.

Mike and Kathy Jelliffe of Nenge Books have once again provided all the support I have needed to have this book published and printed. Their usual patience, expertise and integrity are like gold.

All the people mentioned above have truly blessed me by their willingness to work so hard behind the scenes. I thank God for each of you. I am so very grateful to God for the provision of my garden, which constantly gives me hugs of beauty as I delight in the visits from some of His wonderful creations.

Juvenile Blue-faced Honeyeater

Introduction

*I*f you have already visited my garden by reading my first book, *A Garden of Simple Delights & Profound Truths,* then welcome back! A special welcome to you if this is your first visit. I hope you enjoy it.

By way of introduction, the draft of the first book was written in one week during a COVID-19 lockdown in 2021. With the exception of a dragonfly, it featured the more permanent residents of the garden, namely the flowers, trees and shrubs.

My garden just keeps on giving. It has plenty to display and share. This new book, *Come, See & Wonder,* once again finds its roots in my garden. It is a collection of memories, stories and photos of my encounters with my garden visitors over the past ten years.

The motivation to write this sequel was threefold. Firstly, but not primarily, it was to give purpose to my growing love of writing. Secondly, to introduce you to a very small selection of the countless and diverse visitors to my garden, and to tell the stories of our encounters with each other. The third and most important motivation was my deep desire to share with you how God, my Heavenly Father, has used each interaction to reveal to me more simple delights and profound truths of His character and the splendour of His Creation.

As I wrote, I wanted to get to know more about the appearance, habitat and behaviour of each garden visitor. My bird books and the Internet were handy sources of information.

Sometimes, the facts were so numerous and so interesting, it was tempting to include as many as possible in each chapter. I had to remind myself that I was not writing an ornithological tome or a field study book. To avoid overshadowing the intended story with facts and figures, I have included a separate list of websites that I have found most interesting. You may like to explore these.

It is my prayer that as you read this book you will accept the invitation to come, see and wonder at what these garden visitors reveal, and then join with the hymn writer acknowledging:

Eastern Rosella

All things bright and beautiful,
    All creatures great and small,
All things wise and wonderful:
    The Lord God made them all.

Each little flow'r that opens,
    Each little bird that sings,
He made their glowing colours,
    He made their tiny wings.

He gave us eyes to see them,
And lips *[pens and computers]* that we might tell,
    How great is God Almighty,
    Who has made all things well.

Mrs Cecil F. Alexander[4] [brackets mine]

Prologue

A garden intrinsically extends an invitation to both humans and members of the animal kingdom alike. The invitation is not only for the birds, animals and insects to come and find enjoyment, shelter and sustenance, but also for humans. The invitation is to come, see and wonder at what God has created, and be amazed and blessed.

The majority of visitors to my garden do not enter through an open gate, nor do they come by an official invitation or appointment. Neither do they break the laws of trespassing. The majority fly in, while others squeeze under the gates, boundary fences or through the bushes. Some visitors have claimed the garden as part of their territory while others are seasonal visitors, having migrated from afar. They all come at the perpetual invitation of the garden itself.

From dawn to dusk they come, and some, such as bats and bandicoots, come at night. I never know who will be visiting or how many! That is not a problem because I don't have to cook a meal or prepare the guest room. Within my garden is some thick foliage that provides shelter for the birds to build their nests and raise their families safely in its depths. My gardener, Julio, intentionally chooses plants and flowers that will attract the visiting creatures and provide a constant smorgasbord of goodies such as seeds, nectar, and pollen, for them to enjoy.

It is the humans who must come via the gate. Any stranger who comes through my gate needs to ring the doorbell, prove their identity and establish their credentials before being granted permission to enter my yard or house. My family and friends of course have a permanent open invitation.

Gardens are important to God. In the Bible[5] we read of God planting a garden in the east, in Eden. There He placed Adam and Eve to tend the garden and also to enjoy its pleasures. We read that the Lord God walked in the garden in the cool of the day. It was His delight.

A garden also invites us to employ every one of our senses during the visit. In my garden there could be the scent of a rose, the taste of a succulent passionfruit, a tiny lizard seen scurrying for cover, a bird heard chirping in a tree or a rose thorn ready to prick a careless human.

If you have read my first book, you may remember that my garden is a wrap-around garden, surrounding the house. Each window allows a view of some aspect of the garden, giving opportunities to keep a close-up watch on some of the visitors as they come and go, particularly the feathered variety. Other visitors I have met, literally face to face, as they peek in from the outside. The windows act as a handy barrier between the visitor and myself without lessening the impact of the interaction - as long as I am still and quiet. However, there was the one visitor that I wish to never see anywhere in my garden ever again.

I now invite you, via the pages of this book, to visit my garden, meet a selection of my garden visitors and be in wonder and awe at God's creation. The simple delights and profound truths will be revealed.

Black-faced Cuckoo-shrike

The Circus in the Tree

Rainbow Lorikeet in flight

*I*t happened in an instant. A high-pitched screech, flashes of colour, a whoosh of wings and the click of my camera. In that split second I managed to capture the moment a colourful rainbow lorikeet zoomed past my head at lightning speed. Suddenly… the tree was empty and silent.

It wasn't until I retreated to the house that the scout birds returned to the highest branches, looking, looking.... The moment they sounded the 'all clear' screech the remainder of the rainbow lorikeet flock rerurned to their 'restaurant' in the bottlebrush tree.

The birds disappeared into the tree, bedecked in their God-designed, brilliantly coloured plumage of orange-red, yellow, bluish mauve and green. The gaudy costumes of circus clowns or trapeze artists pale into insignificance in contrast. The green back feathers blend with the green foliage providing instant camouflage as they get their bearings and search for food that takes their fancy. Here and there stunning flashes of colourful feathers appear as the birds twist and turn as they emerge from their camouflage in the tree, then disappear again. This requires some skilful moves. Their flexible little bodies are perfectly designed by God for flying and feeding with acrobatic stunts included!

Rainbow lorikeets have insatiable appetites. They have established flight paths along which they fly high and fast daily in their constant search for food. The seasonal abundance of bright red bottlebrush flowers in particular is like a beacon guiding them to a plentiful banquet just waiting for their delight.

Dining is a noisy multi-skilled activity! There is a background of screeching and chattering, as they incessantly communicate with their mate and others in the flock. They

Hungry Rainbow Lorikeet

keep a constant lookout for danger as they search for the most luscious nectar-filled flower spikes the tree has to offer.

Without a safety harness or a net, they plop, sway, and bounce their way along a branch to reach those delicious spikes. They use their God-designed sharp beak and feet, consisting of two toes forward and two toes back, to carry out their moves with consummate agility. It takes a whole lot of neck-bending, stretching, hanging upside down, somersaulting, twisting and turning, all the while clinging tenaciously to the last centimetres of the branch. Once there, they feast on the nectar and pollen using their brush tipped tongue. All this they do unaware that they are putting on an amazing acrobatic performance. No wonder they have earned the reputation of being the 'feathered clowns of the garden'.

If, by chance, there is a miscalculation in landing and a freefall occurs, a few very fast wing beats propel the supple bird up the right way to rejoin its rambunctious troupe. A human acrobat would quake in their shoes.

Meanwhile, as I watch from the porch, one minute I am laughing heartily, and the next I'm holding my breath or gasping with astonishment. Suddenly and unpredictably the show is over and with screeches and multiple flashes of colour, the feathered clowns are gone on whirring wings. Again I am left in silence to ponder.

My mind turns to God, the Creator. How amazing is His creativity! God must have had so much pleasure creating rainbow lorikeets; choosing the vibrant colours and designing such a wonderful purpose-built body for them.

As I laugh out of enjoyment at their antics, I have a suspicion that God is laughing and enjoying the circus too. Why wouldn't God laugh? Why wouldn't God enjoy watching His creation having fun? After all, part of His nature is happiness and joy.

We humans would not have a sense of humour if God didn't have a sense of humour in the first place!

The Bible says;
  'So God created mankind in his own image,
    in the image of God he created them'
          Genesis 1:27 (NIV)

So, whenever the Circus in the Tree comes to my garden, God and I have a laugh together.

Upside down Lorikeet

The Dapper Little Gent

My electric toothbrush hummed away as the bristles did their work. To me there is something relaxing about simultaneously guiding a vibrating toothbrush around my mouth and wandering around the house at the same time. I formed this habit during my working life as a teacher, where one hand worked the toothbrush and the other continued to pack my workbasket full of the books and the various odds and ends I would need for a day in the classroom. Now in retirement, the habit continues. It is a signal that breakfast is over and it's time to start the day in earnest.

The first of my morning rituals (even before coffee!) is to go through the house opening the windows and doors, drawing back the verticals and some curtains as well. I don't always bother to include every room in this routine, but on this particular morning I did. I had already passed by the guest room, but then was inexplicably drawn back into it. Walking in, I just could not believe my eyes and froze a few steps from the window!

I carefully silenced the electric toothbrush, which still filled my mouth, and wished I could instantly exchange it for my camera. I was utterly transfixed but knew that if I moved, I would spoil an incredibly special moment. Growing directly outside that window is a bottlebrush tree. Its stunted, thin foliage combines sufficiently with the neighbour's palm trees to provide an effective privacy screen, hiding the neighbour's backyard and the street from view. It also forms a handy, quiet little retreat for the visiting birds.

On a branch of the stunted bottlebrush tree sat a diminutive wren, its long tail cocked high, pitch black except for a brilliant crimson-red blotch on its back and with very dark grey/brown wing feathers. Because of the richness of the colours I assumed this bird to be a male. This tiny feathered gent was enjoying a quiet solitary moment, shielded from behind by a curtain of leaves. This place was five-star rated as it also provided him a handy window that reflected his image. Wrens just love places with reflective surfaces where they can admire themselves, or be deluded into thinking the reflection is a rival, or another of its kind.

It was obvious that this wren was feeling completely relaxed. He was so engrossed in his preening routine that he was totally unaware of my presence. I too was engrossed as I watched him use his short pointy beak to preen his wings and tail feathers. Each feather was meticulously attended to while clinging onto a twig with tiny feet that were fitted with razor sharp claws, custom made by the Creator. When it came to dealing with those hard to reach places, one fragile spindly leg was able to bear his body weight, whilst the other scratched various places at high speed. Not one place would be missed, nor would there be a feather out of place, so by the time he had finished he was quite the dapper little gent!

As I watched, I thanked God for this unique, up close and personal encounter with such a spectacular member of His creation. I marvelled at how God endowed so much beauty on such a tiny delicate bird. Suddenly, I was jolted back to reality. I needed the bathroom sink! Alas, when I returned, to my great disappointment, the delightful little visitor was gone.

Now I was inquisitive. I wanted to know more about my tiny visitor. My bird books and the Internet informed me that the dapper little gent's real identity is a Red-backed Fairy-wren. In spite of a long name, this little wren and his kin are Australia's smallest of the fairy-wrens and weigh about eight grams. He was a breeding male because only males of that status are decked out in their very best red and black 'bib and tucker', exactly as my little friend was that special morning. Non-breeding males and females are very similar—both are pale brownish birds with brown tails.[6]

Ah! That could be a clue as to what this little wren was up to. His fastidious preening could be for some amorous intent! But then again, my romantic imagination may have been running away with me and he was just having his morning preen.

There is so much I do not know about these little wrens that inhabit the dense underbrush in northern and eastern Australia. But, what I do know is this: that on this day, God knew that His Red-backed Fairy wren was in the little bower outside my guest room window enjoying a quiet solitary moment. How do I know this?

Jesus said;

"Are not two sparrows sold for a penny?

Yet not one of them will fall to the ground outside your Father's care."

Matthew 10:29 (NIV)

If God knows where each of the common and numerous sparrows are, He also knows where His red-backed fairy-wrens are too. My Heavenly Father knows where I am as well. That's loving security!

What's more, being drawn into the guest room was not as inexplicable as it seemed, but rather God's intentional invitation to come and see His exquisite little Red-backed Fairy-wren. I did not deserve the special treatment of a personal viewing. It was because He loves me and knows what I love and what I enjoy that He bestowed on me this unique touch of grace.

Not only did I learn about this dear little wren, I learnt a lot about our incredible God who;

"... determines the number of the stars and calls them each by name."

Psalm 147:4 (NIV)

Yet, He delights in delighting His children and calls them by name.

God has another even more pressing invitation; to come and see and wonder about Jesus, His Son, to discover who He is and to get to know Him by reading the Bible.

"…give the Lord a chance to show you how good He is."

Psalm 34:8 (ERV)

Red-backed Fairy-wren - (the Dapper Little Gent)

Face to Face

On yet another day a nonchalant wander into my bedroom came to an abrupt halt. There, on my windowsill was a face that only a mother could love. The sheer curtains enabled both of our faces to stare at each other in relative privacy. The face looking at me belonged to an Eastern Water Dragon!

Many Common Garden Skinks (Penny Lizards) reside in my garden but unfortunately, Blue-tongue Lizards are only very occasional visitors. To my knowledge this eastern water dragon was the first and largest lizard to ever visit my garden.

The dragon must have sensed my presence because he showed me his wide open mouth in an attempt to scare me off. I stood my ground behind the curtain and took the rare opportunity for an up close and personal inspection of an Eastern Water Dragon's throat. A strange and fascinating sight! I'm sure I saw what he had for breakfast!

Beyond that gaping red mouth and throat, I could see most of its head and front feet. It seemed to be wearing a crest that looked like a helmet of enlarged pointy scales.[7] The powerfully built front feet wielding long sharp claws clung menacingly on the brick windowsill. The little bit of the body I could see was covered with rough scales and sharp spines which were of grey or brown colours. A patch of red on the bit of underbelly that was just visible declared it to be a male.[8]

It was time to find the camera for a photographic session. Slowly I withdrew from the window and beat a hasty retreat

A (too young for mascara?) Juvenile Eastern Water Dragon

to the backdoor and cautiously into the garden. What a sight greeted me! There was a mature water dragon, stretched to its full length along the windowsill, luxuriating in the sun. It fitted perfectly on the one-metre-long windowsill. What really amazed me was its very long tail, which is apparently two-thirds the length of the entire lizard. Now I could see the continuation of the spines down the back to the tip of the tail and the rest of its markings and colours; black bands on the back and tail, and a long black stripe that started behind the eye and continued down the side of the head. It looked like badly applied mascara!

It was no mean feat to not frighten the reptile as I simultaneously edged closer and closer to inspect this unusual visitor while preparing to take a photo. Finally, it was time to pause and press the camera's shutter. But, within that instant of resting the thumb on the button and exerting pressure, the whole one metre of lizard disappeared, never to be seen again.

Little did I know, that a couple of years later I was to have another encounter with a face that only a mother could love.

… I froze in absolute astonishment! There on the windowsill was a bird, the like of which I had never seen before. Its wide-open cavernous mouth, surrounded by some downy feathers, took on an extra ghoulish appearance as its face was squashed hard against the window when it crash landed on the windowsill. This strange, feathered creature truly had a face only a mother could love. It was only a momentary interaction but a memorable privilege to see one of God's unusual creatures so up close and personal.

While I was finding my camera, the bird had managed to manoeuvre itself from the windowsill and had somehow landed in the neighbour's yard. Judging by the feeble attempts to fly, this strange bird was still finding its newly acquired urge to fly a challenge. After numerous aborted take-offs and more spectacular belly flops, the novice flier finally achieved some brief moments of flight. This diligent practice continued in the neighbour's garden for some time, then the bird disappeared never to be seen again.

The memory of that face squashed against my kitchen window remained and I continued to be curious about this strange bird. An internet search not only identified this face but also described features that I missed seeing due to the fleeting nature of its visit.

So, behind that face with the gaping mouth was a juvenile Eastern Koel. Both the juvenile and its mother share similar colouring and patterns of plumage. The patterns alternate in shades of dark browns and creamy-buff. What distinguishes the juvenile is the dark colouring on its head. As I read on I discovered that the eastern koels have quite a story. That's for later as I have another story to share with you now.

As I wrote about the previous encounters with the two faces that only a mother could love, a profound experience I had about twenty-five years ago came to my mind.

The Christian weekend retreat was drawing to a close. As a group leader, I was leading my group's debrief session. One woman confessed to the group that on the first night when the groups were being formed, she looked around and wondered who would be in her group. She saw someone who she considered to be the owner of the most unusual face that she had ever seen. She also admitted that she had hoped she wasn't to be in the same group as that person. Well, surprise! She was! But this women wasn't finished yet...

She went on to say that over the weekend God had worked in her life and taught her many things. She eventually settled in and began to enjoy being in that group. She learnt to look beyond the face that was on the other side of the table, and started to get to know the person who owned the face, and, to never judge a book by its cover!

I was gobsmacked to say the least! This disclosure was beyond the pale. It was my face she was referring to! Please don't rush for the tissues yet, but read on. Remaining composed, I was able to forgive her and pray a blessing over her as the session finished.

As afternoon tea was being served, I took the opportunity to hightail it to the bathroom in the dormitory. I needed to be alone with my Maker. I was ever so thankful that God had done some deep work in my life a couple of years previously. I learnt to become comfortable and accepting of who I was and Whose I was.

As I looked face to face and eye to eye with the reflection in the mirror, there I saw my face that was dearly loved by my mother and father and loved infinitely more dearly by my Heavenly Father. In fact, He formed my face out of my parents' genes. I remembered again a lovely Bible verse;

"For you created my inmost being;

You knit me together in my mother's womb.

I praise you because I am fearfully and wonderfully made."

Psalm 139:13-14. (NIV)

The face in the mirror reflected this absolutely amazing truth; not only did the Creator and Sustainer of the universe love my face, He loved me, the total ME, body, mind soul and spirit. He loved me so deeply that He sent His only Son, Jesus to die on the cross for all my sins so I could become a child of God. The Bible explains it like this:

"Yet to all who did receive Him,

to those who believed in His name,

He gave the right to become children of God."

John 1:12 (NIV)

I rejoined the group with my head held high and a smile on my face knowing I was genuinely and deeply loved and cherished no matter what!

'Wattle' They Do Next?

*I*t was February 2021. There was not a breath of wind. The heavens opened yet again to release another deluge of rain, thoroughly drenching anyone and anything that did not have a raincoat, umbrella or a place to shelter. The gutters were overflowing almost the full length of the house. From my vantage point at the window, it was as if I was looking out from behind a waterfall. Then as quickly as it started, the rain ceased, leaving stuffy humid weather behind until the next downpour.

This stubborn weather event was going nowhere. The native animals and birds (and people) would be doing it tough. The ground was thoroughly water-logged and trees struggled to provide adequate shelter. I was glad that God had endowed birds with ways of waterproofing their feathers.

I had become aware that a family of Little Wattlebirds, also known as the Brush Wattlebird, was nesting somewhere in the vines on the back fence of the house, but I had no success in finding the nest. Then the rains came…

One morning, as I was standing at the window looking out at the drenched and soggy world, the Little Wattlebird family arrived. There was one parent and two fledglings. The canny wattlebird parent carefully hunkered down its young in the same tree that the dapper little gent had visited. This tree had a mixture of perching options available, enough for multiple occupants. When the fledglings were settled, the parent left them, no doubt to get food. I was fascinated.

Adult Little Wattlebird

'Wattle' they do next? I asked myself.

During the day I kept returning to the window to check on the feathered family. Those two fledglings seemed to sense what was required of them and they obediently waited and waited… As the day wore on a pattern emerged. The parents were never far away. As well as constantly making food deliveries, they seemed to sense when those heavy downpours were about to drop yet another watery load. One parent would always arrive before the rain fell, to keep their young safe while the rain tumbled down around them. While they waited for the rain to stop, the parent took the opportunity to teach their young to preen and oil their feathers. Occasionally, when the parent felt that it was safe, they would encourage the young to leave their inner shelter and move to the edge of the tree and stretch their wings. They were always guided back by one of the parents before the next deluge arrived.

Between downpours there was a lot of coming and going as the parents took turns in satisfying their permanently hungry offspring. These birds are nectar feeders. I began to wonder how the dreadful weather would affect all the birds that relied on nectar for their daily sustenance. My research revealed that heavy rain can indeed wash nectar away from many plants and flowers.

It wasn't long before I discovered how these Little Wattlebirds solved the problem. A couple of metres from their shelter tree was my neighbour's very tall pawpaw tree, loaded with fruit. Some fruit was showing evidence of having been eaten, presumably by fruit bats that often made their presence heard at night. Imagine my surprise when I saw one of the parents flying to and fro from the pawpaw tree, stuffing pawpaw flesh into its mouth, then poking it down the mouths of their young. What a gourmet meal; fresh, soft, and juicy!

'Wattle' they think of next?

As long as the rain event continued, this hiding and feeding routine was re-enacted daily. I pondered the ingenuity that these parents showed in caring for their young in such inclement weather. How did they know how to choose such real estate, where my fence and house added to their shelter and security? They had certainly been astute in finding such shelter with plenty of room, easy access for parental visits, food deliveries and emergency departures.

Also, how did the parent birds know when the next deluge was imminent? Just maybe they, like us humans, can sometimes sense rain coming. But the other amazing thing was that their timing was exact. They always reached their offspring before the rain fell, thus giving the youngsters safety and security.

I was puzzled as to how and why these nectar feeding birds sometimes varied their diet with insects, berries, and seeds, and discovered that pawpaw was such good food? Was it due to pre-knowledge passed down through the ages or could it be the tantalising sweet aroma of the pawpaw? Or, were they just driven by hunger due to the lack of nectar and decided to taste test it? In due course I was to find out. The answer was astonishing.

'Wattle' they eat next?

My thoughts turned to the two fledglings, whose obedience was consistently without fault.

Day by day, deluge by deluge, those two little birds just hunkered down on whatever branch their parents chose. There they sat, patiently, trustingly, waiting; totally dependent on their parents to come and tend all their needs. Their survival depended on their absolute obedience. How could these 'children' be so good for so long? Every parent and teacher would love to know their secret!

Eventually, the weather event began to move away. The patches of sunshine became more frequent and the rain eased. This was the cue for the wattlebird parents to lead their family to the outer branches of their shelter tree. Now they were able to soak up the feeble sunshine. Finally, a beautifully clear sunny day dawned and the wattlebird family left the shelter tree forever.

Where did they go? 'Wattle' they do next?

I'll never be able to give a precise scientific answer to these questions, but this I do know, these Little Wattlebirds were created by God. He lovingly endowed them with an incredible instinct that drives their behaviour, their parenting, and their feeding, thus enabling them to survive and thrive in their natural environment.

What a lovely picture of parental love and care on show. If these little birds care so diligently for their family, how much more does God love and care for us? He truly is an amazing God!

Obedient juvenile Little Wattlebirds

Juvenile's Story

The Counterfeit Finds Love

A most ludicrous feeding activity was being played out right before my eyes. I would have missed the exhibition if I had not gone to investigate the commotion that had so abruptly and unexpectedly shattered my peaceful autumn afternoon. There, sitting high and conspicuous in the neighbour's loquat tree, was another young Eastern Koel. It was over two years since the first youngster had appeared at my kitchen window. A loud incessant cheeping was coming from its cavernous mouth. All and sundry were left in no doubt that its owner was ravenously hungry..

I was surprised to discover that a Little Wattlebird was feeding this demanding young Eastern Koel that was almost four times its size! Crazy! Why this unusual behaviour?

Over the next three weeks this feeding routine continued in various neighbourhood trees, including my big bottlebrush tree. Then one day I was surprised to see this huge young koel alone in the foliage of the bottlebrush tree near my dining room window. Did the youngster have a crash landing into the branches while refining its flying skills? Had the wattlebird and the young koel formed some sort of unique bond like we see on television at times? Or, just maybe the Little Wattlebird was exhibiting (like its relatives in the previous chapter) its proven parenting skills of shepherding youngsters into a safe place, while it went to check out what cuisine was available

Feeding time

in the neighbourhood? Just what was the connection between these two very different birds?

Now my curiosity was rekindled. Further research revealed some very surprising information. My first surprise was to discover that since childhood I have been familiar with the male of the species but not under its official name, of Eastern Koel. My family called it the storm bird, and others called it the rain bird. This bird, with its multiple identities, gained its notoriety from his annoying repetitious call of 'storm' that drives the residents of eastern Australia crazy throughout each spring and summer.

My second surprise was to learn that this bird, which by now I had named 'Juvenile', is a member of the wider cuckoo clan that has quite a story as a migratory counterfeit. I finally solved the conundrum of why an Eastern Koel is being fed by a Little Wattlebird!

This is Juvenile's story…

After wintering in south-east Asia, Juvenile's relations make their annual migration to breed in eastern Australia. The males and females arrive separately. They have a common purpose; to execute a plan of distraction and deception in order to find a suitable nest in which to lay an egg that would be incubated and raised by another bird.

Being migratory birds, they return to the same locality for their annual summer sojourn. The first to arrive are the males, resplendent in their lustrous black feathers shot with blue and green, and contrasting striking eyes. While awaiting the arrival of the females, the males are kept busy checking out the real estate, the food supply, and the neighbours. Eastern Koels are fruit eaters and are especially fond of native figs and berries. They supplement their diet with protein rich insects at nesting time. Their real estate preference is for the nests built by friarbirds, wattlebirds, and figbirds.[9]

As the females arrive in their plumage of dark browns and creamy-buff, the males attempt to attract them with the relentless call, "Storm! Storm!". The males and females do not mate for life, so it is imperative to quickly find a mate. Having made their hasty choice, each couple sets to work in tandem to execute their cunning plan to add to the Eastern Koel population. They squawk a duet in an unsynchronised cacophony of sound.[10] This puts the other species of nesting birds in the area into such a panic that they desert their nests. Now the pair can search for the best real estate on offer without distraction. The male then varies his call to keep the other birds in panic mode. Meanwhile, the female carries out her part of the deception and carefully chooses her ready-made nest. There she deposits her single egg. Juvenile's egg was laid in a Little Wattlebird's nest.

When the rightful nest owners return to their nests, they find there is an extra egg there. Somehow they fail to notice the deception. Thus, the sadly deluded foster parents diligently and with tender loving care, carry out the incubation and nesting duties for an expanded clutch of eggs. Once hatched, Juvenile, the counterfeit nestling, grows fast. He forces the other genuine occupants out of the nest, if they had not already perished for lack of food and attention.

When it is time for Juvenile to leave the nest, his foster parents continued the full time job of feeding this large bird that is not their own. After all, going through the phase of being permanently hungry and growing new feathers is normal for most birds. But, unbeknown to the foster parents, Juvenile, was eating up big and bulking up in preparation for a very long flight he was destined to take in the not so distant future.

As I watched the foster parents frenetically feeding their charge in my garden, some questions came to my mind. At the top of my list was; how could these foster parents be so deceived as to not recognise their own flesh and blood? Another was; why did God create a species of birds such as the cuckoo and koel and others who rely on other species to raise their young?[11]

God knew what He was doing and why when He created some birds with strange habits. God knows best.

"For my thoughts are not your thoughts,
  neither are your ways my ways, declares the Lord.
As the heavens are higher than the earth
  so are my ways higher than your ways…"

Isaiah 55:8 (NIV)

Now, back in my garden, I looked upon the ludicrous feeding activities with different eyes. I see something special happening. Duped though they may have been, Juvenile's foster parents were tirelessly displaying undeserved love to this overgrown bird that had become their lot to care for and treat as their very own. This called for sacrifice driven by undeserved love.

From sunrise to sunset they would search for food. The foster parents would prefer to suck nectar, but somehow they knew that Juvenile needed protein-rich insects. The 'somehow' was a God given instinct. He knew exactly what Juvenile needed for that long trip ahead of him. So, the foster parents sacrificed their natural food and hunted insects constantly. They relentlessly shoved the insects down Juvenile's cavernous mouth. Love sacrifices. Yes, they had certainly developed a unique bond.

But the bond was soon to break. Time was moving on. The day was coming when there would be no more ludicrous feeding activities in my garden. It was time for Juvenile to learn how to be a real Eastern Koel, not a counterfeit wattlebird. It was time for him to look after himself and be Juvenile by name only. It was time too for his foster parents to reclaim their identity as Little Wattlebirds and get on with life as 'empty nesters' for now.

Autumn had arrived. It was time for the migratory yen to stir in Juvenile's heart. How could this inexperienced bird find its way to south-east Asia?

God had this covered too! According to some unconfirmed observations,[12] Juvenile's biological parents would actually show up again! They would return to the vicinity of the nests where they had earlier laid their eggs! The possible reason given for this twist is to provide Juvenile with the unique auditory imprinting needed prior to his migration back north. To me, this is something only God would plan to care for his creation.

Here is another twist! It appears that when Juvenile's real parents re-connect with their young, they will wean him off his foster parents' diet of mainly insects and onto a fruit diet of figs, berries, cherry tomatoes and other fruits![13] This is the koel's preferred and now most needed food. Fully bulked up with protein and sugar fixes, Juvenile is now ready to make his first migratory flight north to winter with his real family in south-east Asia. God thinks of everything!

"Goodbye Juvenile! Fly high in God's care. See you next spring!"

God knows us through and through. He knows exactly who we are. He understands us fully. He knows when we are sad and glad. He knows when we do wrong and make a mess of our lives. He sees the counterfeit in us when we try to be who we are not!

God knows that we need His undeserving love and forgiveness of our sins. He knows we need to discover who we are and Whose we are and, how deeply He loves us with His undeserved love. He also knows that we need peace in our hearts and joy in our souls. God thinks of everything! So He sent Jesus, to be our Saviour and friend, to imprint His love on our hearts.

Hungry 'Juvenile' Eastern Koel and Little Wattlebird

The Rescue Mission

Next door, in what was the two-storey house I grew up in, a commotion had erupted. The sound of voices raised in surprise and excitement drifted down into my house. The excited tone and volume of the voices kept rising. Because of the closeness of both houses it was not uncommon to hear the background hum of neighbours' voices, heard but not listened to. Whatever was happening, it was not my business.

Unexpectedly my name sounded out amongst the chorus of exclamations. Now, it was certainly my business! I went out the back door and looked up. The neighbours were peering down, pointing and exclaiming; "There's a snake in your hedge!" My heart missed a beat or three! A snake! In my hedge! I was horrified and frightened. Why? I just do not like snakes!

Someone upstairs had spotted this legless reptile weaving its uninvited way across the top of my Lilly Pilly hedge. So intent was it on finding a place to enjoy the late afternoon spring sunshine that the voices raised in alarm did not distract this slithery reptile from its quest.

This family were good neighbours. They were not given to intruding eyes even though their verandah overlooked my property. However, on this particular afternoon, I was very glad that they had seen, and I had heard.

There certainly was no room in my garden for me and a snake. Someone was going to have to expel that creature from my property and I wasn't volunteering!

A scenario flashed through my mind of not ever being able to freely wander in my garden, knowing that, that slithery, beady-eyed, tongue flicking, legless reptile could be lurking with intent! It had to go, and the sooner the better! A number of locations crossed my mind; Perth, Darwin… Anywhere, far away from me and my garden as possible!

My neighbour could see that I was heading for a meltdown and that would achieve nothing, so she bravely volunteered for relocation duties. In no time at all she appeared in my garden with her colour co-ordinated tools of trade and her muscular male friend as backup. With the confidence of a professional snake whisperer, she began. Barehanded, she grabbed the end of the snake's tail and pulled. The snake was not at all impressed with the rude interruption to its planned afternoon of sun baking, so it entwined itself tightly around

The Snake Whisperer in action

the branches. Finally, it relinquished its hold and out it came. Rescue complete!

The neighbourly snake whisperer deemed it a fine specimen of a harmless Diamond Python. I acknowledged that it was indeed one of God's creations and chose not to comment any further. I breathed a sigh of relief as the snake whisperer and her friend left my garden carrying the snake in a tub to a new location. I had been rescued!

The Diamond Python

Later that evening as I replayed the event in my mind, I remembered another garden and another snake. It was the Garden of Eden, the first dwelling place of Adam and Eve. The Biblical account is to be found in the opening chapters of Genesis.

This incredibly beautiful, peaceful and harmonious garden was where all the creatures and Adam and Eve freely roamed. It was the place where God chose to walk in the cool of the evening and talk with Adam and Eve.

Suddenly, one day, a honey-smooth, inviting, cajoling, convincing unfamiliar voice was being heard at the Tree of Knowledge. This was the only tree from which God had forbidden Adam and Eve to ever eat the fruit from. To do so, would have disastrous consequences. The strange voice was that of a serpent, smooth-talking Eve into doubting God and pressuring her to eat the fruit of the Tree of Knowledge. This was in blatant disobedience to God's instruction. Eve acquiesced, took a bite, and then passed it onto Adam, who succumbed to the temptation of both Eve and the serpent.

Instantaneously things changed. Adam and Eve were reaching for fig leaves to cover themselves. They hid when they heard God walking in the garden in the cool of the day, for they were ashamed of their nakedness. Found out, Adam and Eve invented the blame game. God was having none of that. They both had disobeyed and sinned. They would bear the consequences, as would Satan the serpent.

The Bible records the moment that God spoke to the snake saying:

> *"It will be worse for you. You did this very bad thing… so bad things will happen to you. You must crawl on your belly and eat dust all the days of your life. I will make you and the woman enemies of each other. Your children and her children will be enemies and more!"*
>
> Genesis 3:8 (ERV)

There were ramifications too for Adam and Eve as result of their disobedience. These included pain in childbirth for Eve, and for Adam there would be daily toil for survival. They were expelled from the garden forever. However, before God expelled them from the garden, He lovingly and graciously clothed them in animal skins.

The universal consequences were serious and far-reaching. Humanity's relationship with God had been broken. Sin and death entered the world. But God already had a rescue mission in place! He gave a hint of it when He told the serpent;

> "You will bite her child's foot, but He [Jesus] will crush your head."
>
> Genesis 3:16-19 (NIV)

In the fullness of time, God sent Jesus into the world. A woman gave birth to Him. He would deal the serpent, Satan, the final blow. He would do this by dying on the Cross, offering forgiveness for our sins, the mending of our relationship with God, and defeating death by His Resurrection three days after.

For those who have taken up God's offer of a renewed relationship with Him, death has lost its sting and the grave has been robbed of its victory and all our sins are forgiven.

That day my neighbour was my rescuer from the snake in my garden, however, my fear of snakes remains. But Jesus is the rescuer of my soul. On the cross Jesus died for all my sins and freed me from the fear of death and gave me not only the forgiveness of all my sins, but also eternal life.

Jesus offers to rescue you too. What could this mean for you?

A Simple Delight

What is a simple delight? What is your simple delight? To me, a simple delight is something uncomplicated that brings joy and pleasure. I have a garden full of simple delights, too many to number!

In late 2017 I recorded in my journal my first close encounter with a dove. It was cooing in the Mock Orange Bush outside my kitchen window. Its low, mellow tone gave a sense of peace despite the limited repetitive repertoire. This usually timid and flighty bird was totally unaware of my presence. I was stunned by its close proximity, and was delighted by the simple beauty of this bird.

That very morning in my devotions I had read the account of when Joseph, Mary and the baby Jesus went to the temple in Jerusalem to offer the required sacrifices for Mary's purification and Jesus' consecration.[14] They could only afford the offering designated for the poor of two doves / pigeons[15] (probably similar to one outside my window). It was like putting a face into the story. Then I thought about how Jesus, the Son of God had willingly put aside His Heavenly status to be born into a humble earthly family; who thirty three years later would complete God's rescue mission. He made the ultimate, once and for all sacrifice on the cross, for the sins of the whole world.

There the dove sat, with not a feather out of place, intently calling, calling… I was attracted to its sleek almost satin like plumage. Its head was a muted grey that gradually blended in with the subtle pinkish grey of the throat and under part, which transitioned to a white belly. On each side of a very pointy beak there were beady bright eyes. Around its neck was the distinctive black collar with white spots, hence its name of Spotted Dove. From the nape of the neck to the long brown tail there were various shades of brown. The wings, adorned with a motif that resembled the pattern of a turtle shell gave it its alternative name; Spotted Turtle Dove.

Some years later, I heard a great deal of soft mellow cooing coming once more from the Mock Orange bush. This time, there was a lot of activity as well. A pair of spotted doves were looking for suitable nesting real estate. One little nook took their fancy. They sat on the branch and turned this way and that, testing its size and strength. They carefully checked the nook's opening, which would double as the entrance and exit. The bushy foliage would give seclusion as well as

Pair of doves choosing their nest site

allowing dappled sunlight and fresh airflow, and my house would provide total protection from the hot afternoon sun. The narrow garden path between the bush and the house provided a safe space to enter and exit the nesting nook. No crow or currawong could fit there. The doves would use their ability to rise steeply in flight to exit the nest. The neighbours' huge mango tree would become one of their lookout trees that would give them an expansive view around the immediate neighbourhood.

Having made a prudent choice, the couple set about the process of nest building. They worked like little Trojans to build a flimsy cup of twigs in which to lay two whitish eggs.[16] The nest needed constant renovation due to its fragility. During this process, there was a lot of communication between the dove in the nest and the partner in one of the lookout trees.

Finally came the day when a dove settled on the nest. As both male and female doves are visually alike and both parents do nesting duties, I never knew who was on nest duty. When there was a change of shift, the dove taking up duty would coo a little song. Maybe it was a song of greeting.

Patient parent on nest duty

As the nest was at eye level from within the house, I had kept the sheer curtains drawn and the window shut to avoid sudden movements or loud noises. Gradually I drew back the curtains and opened the window. It was time to introduce myself. Ever so softly I began to talk to them. As I had no idea which dove I was addressing, the one-sided conversation went like this: "Hello Little Mamma, Little Papa!" Later I added "Little Bubbas" every time I went to the window, repeating the greeting over and over. My presence was gradually accepted.

Dove feeding chicks

One warm spring morning there was no bright eye peeping at me from the nest. It was deserted! On closer inspection, I saw two eggs! Clever little mamma! The parent on incubation duty must have known instinctively when it was safe to leave their eggs briefly unattended. Nest duty required endless hours of incredible patience, endurance, and loneliness, to just sit on the nest, come what may.

To be able to have an extra wing stretch and to wiggle their cramped bodies and fly must have been so welcome. In due course the eggs hatched a couple of days apart! 'Meals on wings' were frequently delivered to the nest. One day I was afforded a sneak peek. There they were; two tiny chicks, covered in downy fluff and with faces that only a mother [and father] could love! Bulging eyes yet to open protruded from their little heads. Raised cavernous mouths opened wide, ever hoping it would be their mouth that would get the first and biggest serve of the tasty morsel presented by the attentive parent.

The chicks grew with incredible speed. The parent on feeding duty had to work hard to keep their young fed and safe under their wings. As the chick's down was being replaced by feathers, the chicks began peeping out from under the parental wing and squawking to be fed, yet again!

Who is going first?

The parents were very diligent in educating their young. The most important lesson was learning how to recognise their parents' call. By day there was a lot of repetitious cooing between the parents. During their long hours on the nest I could hear the parent's soft and gentle cooing, in an effort to imprint it on the chick's brain. Maybe, my repetitious conversations were also imprinted?

Day by day the fledglings continued to grow and become more active. They took more interest in their surroundings, often going close to the edge of the nest. Down had given way to feathers. Now there was a lot of wing-flapping and argy-bargy about who was going to be fed first and, who was going over the edge first. One at a time they eventually ventured onto a small branch right beside the nest. Little Mamma/Little Papa were nearby, but not obviously in sight.

At last the big day arrived. The eldest was the first to take its momentous first flight, only to crash-land on my windowsill. After pausing for a few moments to recover from the head knock, it then struggled to the top of the bush to rest until it got its bearings. Then, with the flap of its wings it discovered the freedom of flight. The parents were watching attentively from a nearby perch, calling and encouraging the juvenile to join them.

Spotted Dove on windowsill

The timid one (probably the younger) took a couple more days before it could pluck up courage to leave the nest. A parent would constantly visit the nest and cheer it on. I watched as it finally took flight, crashing onto the windowsill, too afraid to move further.

This was my special simple delight. The young bird was perched up against the window, so close I could have touched it!. I kept talking to it, telling it to be careful out there in the big wide world. I said, 'goodbye' and then prayed for it. Meanwhile, one of the parents was attentively watching this momentous moment unfold from the edge of the gutter a few metres away. Finally it joined its offspring on the windowsill and encouraged it with constant calling and gentle nudging, until the little one finally flapped its wings and took flight.

Now that both juvenile doves had found their wings, the nest lay empty and sad. The parents did not return to the nest as they vary their nesting location. I began to experience a little of the empty nest syndrome. The kitchen seemed so empty with no one to talk to while doing my kitchen duties. Actually, I was surprised just how much I missed that dove family.

A few days later I was sitting on my middle porch reading. Very close by I heard the gentle cooing that I had come to love. I looked up and there were two doves peeping over the gutter; an adult wearing its mark of maturity, the black collar with white spots, and a juvenile with no collar. Immediately, I knew them. As soon as I started talking my 'dove talk' to them they cocked their heads in recognition and then flew away. I am certain that the dove was showing off one of its offspring to me and saying, "Thank you and goodbye". It was a memorable and precious simple delight.

Looking back, I realise that I have had encounters with spotted doves all my life. I used to consider these birds as common, boring, timid brown birds that had a monotonous call. My attitude changed now I've had plenty of time to marvel at how beautifully God has created these doves with their impeccable plumage, their low and mellow cooing and their peaceful persona. It has been a privilege to be able to daily observe and get to know these doves that chose to nest outside my kitchen window. Their presence afforded me many simple delights and revealed some profound truths.

As time went on, I could also see some of God's character reflected in these lovely birds.

"For since the creation of the world, God's invisible qualities - his eternal power and divine nature - have been clearly seen, being understood from what has been made, so that people are without excuse."

Romans 1:20 (NIV)

Jesus strongly encouraged his followers to be as gentle, harmless, and innocent as doves.[17] He was emphasising the peaceable characteristics that are pleasing to Him. Other characteristics are patience, kindness, faithfulness and self-control. I saw the avian expression of these in the dove family outside my kitchen window.

Doves are mentioned in the Bible forty-seven times. Biblical commentators have written much about their significance. Historically, Noah sent a dove out of the ark to find dry land. Romantically, doves feature in the poetic language of some Psalms and the Song of Solomon. Spiritually, their significance is twofold.

Firstly, many of the Bible references are related to their use in sacrifices, and secondly, and most significantly as the representation of the Holy Spirit. The biblical account of Jesus' baptism depicts the Holy Spirit descending upon Him in the form of a dove. The dove symbolises the divine presence, guidance and inspiration provided by the Holy Spirit.[18]

Doves have only one partner for life. The pair form strong bonds and care faithfully for their mates and offspring.[19] This is expressed by building the nest together and sharing the load of nest duties and food gathering. I've already mentioned the endless hours of incredible patience, endurance and loneliness involved in sitting on the nest. They resolutely and diligently remained on nest duty during hail storms, heavy rain events and the searing heat of surrounding bushfires. Why? Instinct, yes, but tempered with dove love.

Peaceful Spotted Dove nesting

There is something very peaceful and calming just looking at a parent dove gently sitting on the nest. No wonder doves have long been linked with peace and harmony and the phrase 'the dove of peace' has become a cliché. However, that peaceful encounter can be easily disturbed. There is a peace that cannot be disturbed ever, and that is the peace of God.

'… the peace of God, which transcends all understanding, will guard your hearts and your minds in Jesus Christ.'

Philippians 4:7 (NIV)

It is the peace that God is inviting you to have. Nothing would delight Him more than for you to invite him into the 'garden of your heart.' [20]

Jesus said:

"Peace I leave with you; my peace I give you.

I do not give to you as the world gives.

Do not let your hearts be troubled and do not be afraid.

John 14:27 (NIV)

"Mercy, peace and love be yours in abundance."

Jude 1:2 (NIV)

41

Interesting Web Sites

- https://ausemade.com.au/flora-fauna/fauna/birds/australasian-wrens-maluridae/red-backed-fairywren-malurus-melanocephalus/
- Plumes of Oz   Eastern Koel as seen in the Hunter Valley NSW.   (Type in Plumes of Oz)
- https://berowrabackyard.com/tag/eastern-koel/https://
- https://www.graemechapman.com.au/library/viewphotos.php?c=310
- https://en.wikipedia.org/wiki/Brood_parasitism
- https://www.coffscoast.com.au/article/sawtell-birdwatching/
- https://hymnsandverses.com/bible-dove-meaning/
- https://margosnotebook.wordpress.com/category/birds-a-f/cuckoos/eastern-koel/
- https://www.animalia.bio/spotted-dove

Endnotes

1. Red-backed Fairy-wren (from original painting by Jennifer Scott, used by permission)
2. Juvenile Eastern Water Dragon. Photo by Kat McKinnoon. I was not able to take my own photo. Too young to wear mascara! See Chapter 'Face to Face'.
3. Photo by Julie Pallant, used by permission.
4. by Mrs Cecil F. Alexander. (https://hymnary.org/text/each_little_flower_that_opens) Public Domain.
5. Refer to Genesis 3:8.
6. https://ebird.org/australia/species/rebfai1/L2038367
7. https://australian.museum/learn/animals/reptiles/water-dragon/
8. https://www.reptilepark.com.au/eastern-water-dragon/
9. https://www.graemechapman.com.au/library/viewphotos.php?c=310
10. ibid
11. https://en.wikipedia.org/wiki/Brood_parasitism
12. https://canberrabirds.org.au/wp-content/uploads/2021/10/CBN-46-2-final.pdf Pages 113 &114
13. Ibid Page 113
14. Luke 2:22-24 When the time came for the purification rites required by the Law of Moses, Joseph and Mary took him to Jerusalem to present him to the Lord (as it is written in the Law of the Lord, "Every firstborn male is to be consecrated to the Lord"[b]), and to offer a sacrifice in keeping with what is said in the Law of the Lord: "a pair of doves or two young pigeons."[c]
15. https://simple.wikipedia.org/wiki/Dove. 'The common names pigeon and dove are often used interchangeably. In ornithology, "dove" tends to be used for smaller species and "pigeon" for larger ones.'
16. https://en.wikipedia.org/wiki/Spotted_dove#:
17. Matthew 10:16 (NIV)
18. https://hymnsandverses.com/bible-dove-meaning/
19. ibid
20. '…You will seek me and find me when you seek me with all your heart. I will be found by you declares the Lord,…" Jeremiah 29:13 &14 (NIV).

www.ingramcontent.com/pod-product-compliance
Lightning Source LLC
Chambersburg PA
CBHW041400160426
42811CB00101B/1492